Pebble® Plus

# How to Build
# Flipsticks

Hands-On
SCIENCE
FUN

by Lori Shores
Consulting Editor: Gail Saunders-Smith, PhD

Consultant: Ronald Browne, PhD
Department of Elementary & Early Childhood Education
Minnesota State University, Mankato

CAPSTONE PRESS
a capstone imprint

Pebble Plus is published by Capstone Press,
151 Good Counsel Drive, P.O. Box 669, Mankato, Minnesota 56002.
www.capstonepub.com

Books published by Capstone Press are manufactured with paper
containing at least 10 percent post-consumer waste.

*Library of Congress Cataloging-in-Publication Data*
Shores, Lori.
 How to build flipsticks / by Lori Shores.
   p. cm.—(Pebble plus. Hands-on science fun)
 Summary: "Simple text and full-color photos instruct readers how to build flipsticks and explain the science behind
the activity"—Provided by publisher.
 Includes bibliographical references and index.
 ISBN 978-1-4296-5292-6 (library binding)
 ISBN 978-1-4296-6213-0 (paperback)
 1. Motion perception (Vision)—Juvenile literature. 2. Flipsticks (Toy)—Experiments—Juvenile literature. 3.
Science—Study and teaching (Preschool)—Activity programs—Juvenile literature. 4. Science—Study and teaching
(Primary)—Activity programs—Juvenile literature. I. Title. II. Series.
 QP493.S56 2011
 612.8'4—dc22                                                        2010024908

**Editorial Credits**
Erika L. Shores, editor; Gene Bentdahl, designer; Sarah Schuette, photo shoot direction; Marcy Morin, scheduler;
    Laura Manthe, production specialist

**Photo Credits**
All photos by Capstone Studio/Karon Dubke, exceot page 17 (brain illustration), Shutterstock/Oguz Aral

## Note to Parents and Teachers

The Hands-On Science Fun series supports national science standards related to physical
science. This book describes and illustrates how to build a flipstick. The images support early
readers in understanding the text. The repetition of words and phrases helps early readers
learn new words. This book also introduces early readers to subject-specific vocabulary words,
which are defined in the Glossary section. Early readers may need assistance to read some
words and to use the Table of Contents, Glossary, Read More, Internet Sites, and Index sections
of the book.

Printed in the United States of America in North Mankato, Minnesota.
092010
005933CGS11

# Table of Contents

*Safety Note:*
Please ask an adult for help in building your flipstick.

# Getting Started

What does this project have
to do with your favorite cartoon?
They both trick your brain
into seeing pictures move!

## Here's what you need:

white paper

2 index cards

pencil

scissors

markers

tape

# Making a Flipstick

Trace an index card
twice on white paper.
Cut out the boxes.

On one piece, draw an alien
with arms at its sides.

On the other piece of paper,

trace the alien except

for the arms.


Draw the alien's arms lifted up.

Use markers to color
the drawings.

Tape the drawings
to the index cards.

Use markers to color
the drawings.

Tape the drawings
to the index cards.

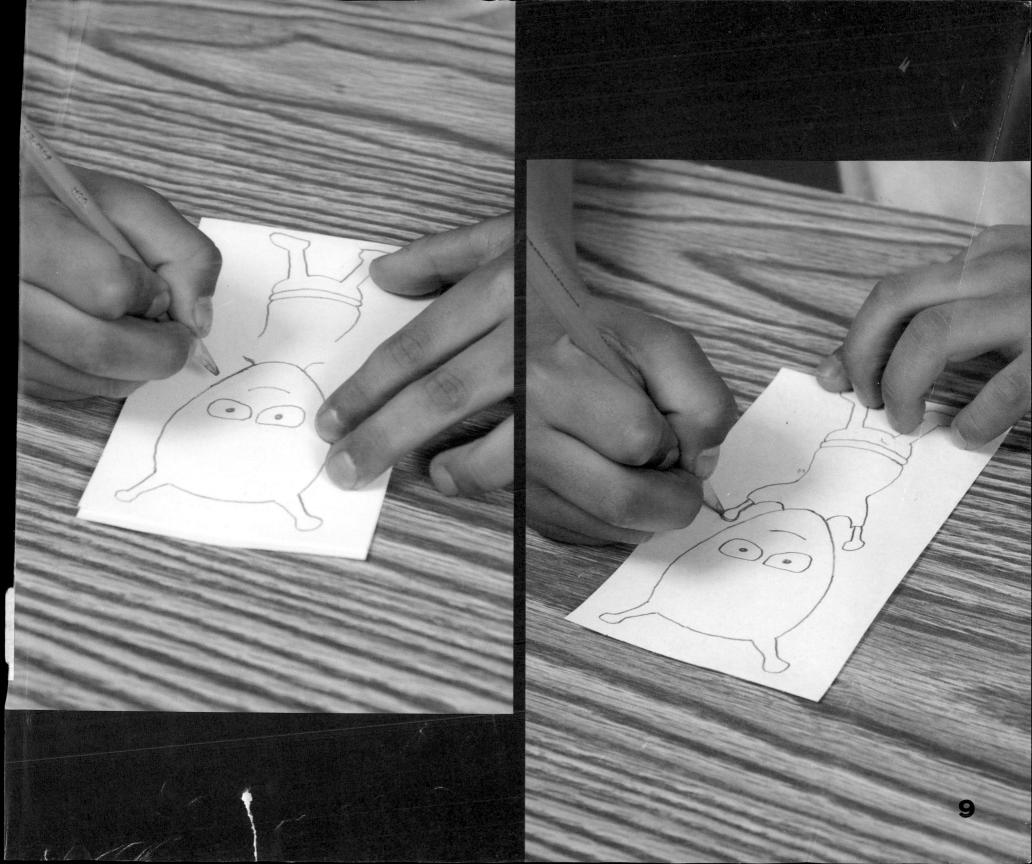

11

Tape the end of the pencil
to the back of one card.

Tape the cards together
with the pencil between them.

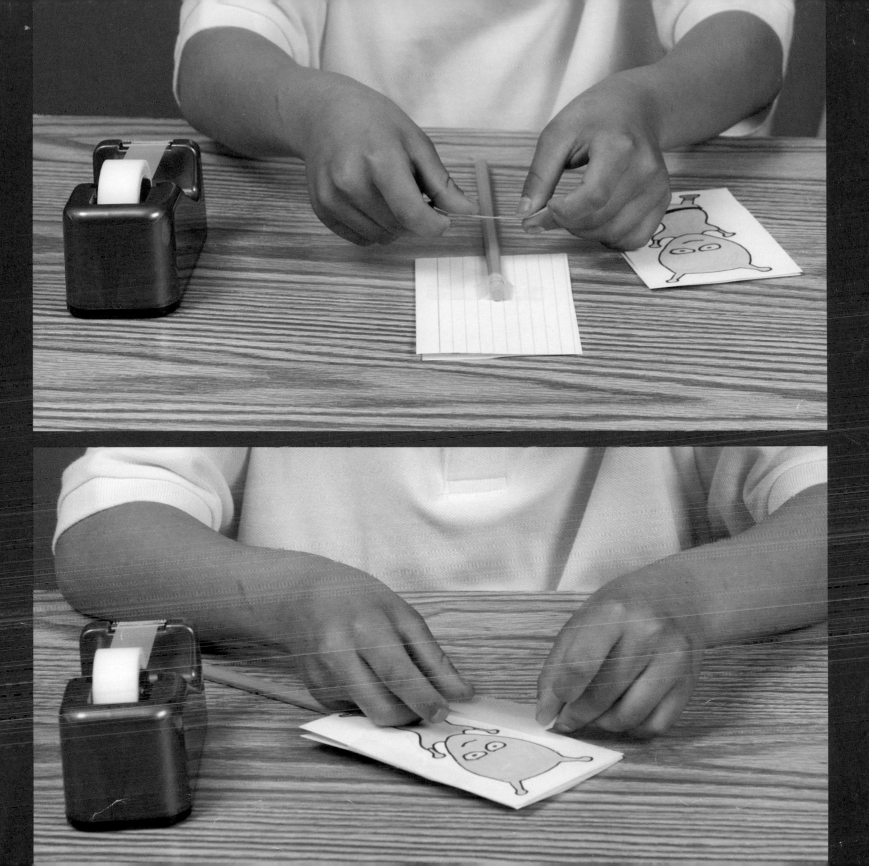

Hold the pencil between your palms.

Rub your hands together to spin the pencil.

What happens?

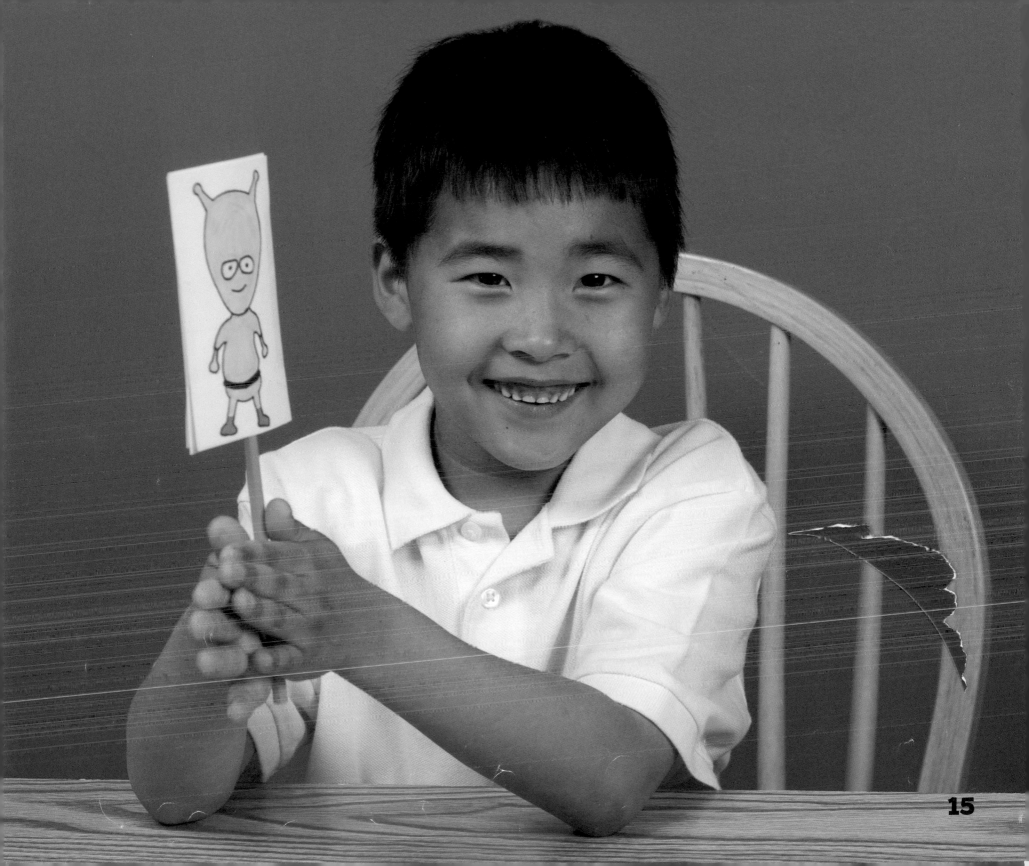

# How Does It Work?

When you look at

a picture, your eyes send

a message to your brain.

When the picture is removed,

your brain remembers it.

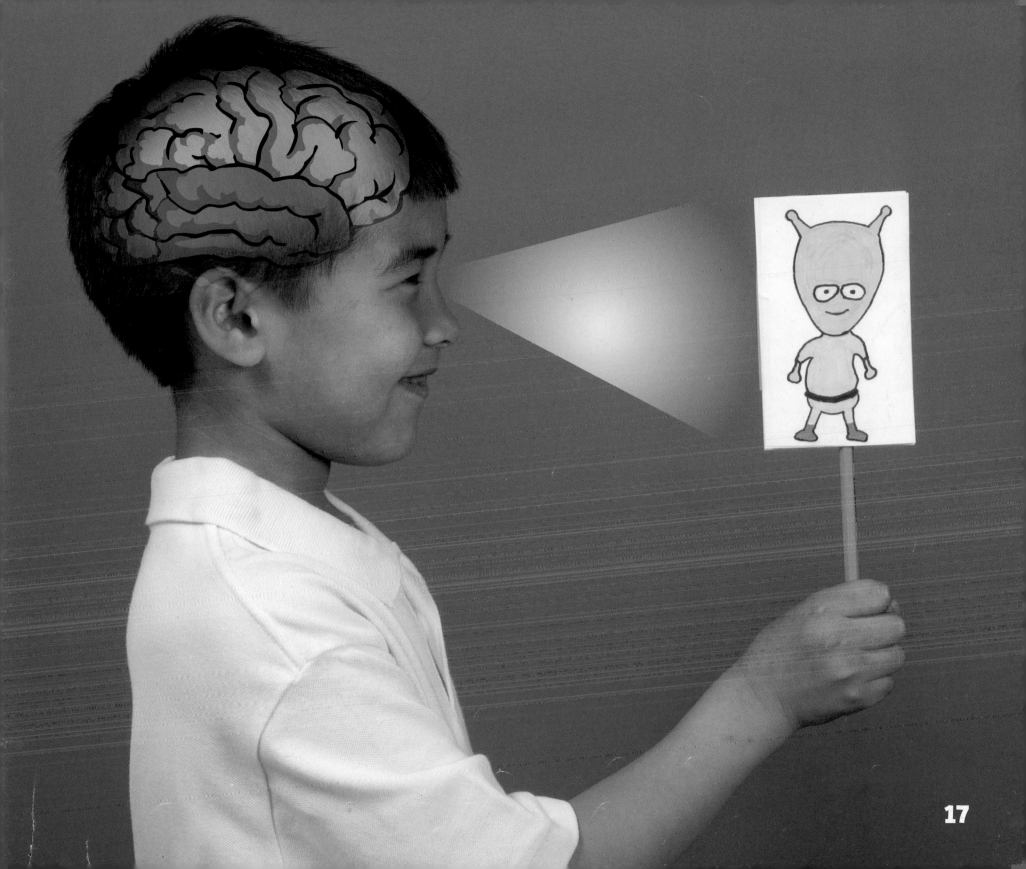

When you see two drawings
quickly, your brain blends
the pictures together.
The two pictures look like
one moving image.

Animated cartoons are made up of many pictures. Each picture is shown for only part of a second. We see the pictures as moving cartoons.

# Glossary

alien—a creature from another planet

animated cartoon—a series of drawings shown very quickly so that they appear to move

project—an assignment that is worked on over a period of time

trace—to copy a picture or shape by following lines seen through a piece of thin paper

# Read More

**Bergin, Mark.** *How to Draw Cartoons.* New York: PowerKids Press, 2011.

**Gardner, Robert.** *Easy Genius Science Projects with Light: Great Experiments and Ideas.* Berkeley Heights, N.J.: Enslow Publishers, 2009.

**Gibson, Gary.** *Light and Color.* Fun Science Projects. Mankato, Minn.: Stargazer Books, 2009.

# Internet Sites

FactHound offers a safe, fun way to find Internet sites related to this book. All of the sites on FactHound have been researched by our staff.

Here's all you do:

Visit *www.facthound.com*

Type in this code: 9781429652926

Check out projects, games and lots more at
**www.capstonekids.com**

**23**

# Index

Word Count: 180
Grade: 1
Early-Intervention Level: 17